M000082322

corrected version

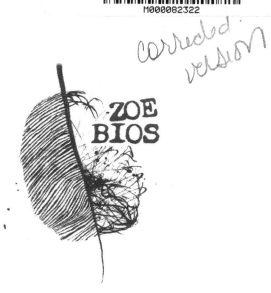

ZOE
BIOS

Is terrorism in our DNA memory?

By Katie Smith

TRAIN OF THOUGHT
PRESS

Publisher's Note

This book is designed to provide information and motivation to our readers. It is sold with the understanding that the publisher is not engaged to render any type of psychological, legal, or any other kind of professional advice. No warranties or guarantees are expressed or implied by the publisher's choice to include any of the content in this volume. Neither the publisher nor the individual author shall be liable for any physical, psychological, emotional, financial, or commercial damages, including, but not limited to, special, incidental, consequential, or other damages. Our views and rights are the same: You are responsible for your own choices, actions, and results.

ISBN: 978-0-9861485-5-2
Library of Congress: 2017937259
TOTP: ZB02082018

Summary: Theory that explains human behavior and specifically the origins and effects of terrorism.

© 2017 by Katie Smith

All rights reserved. No part of this publication may be reproduced, distributed, or transmitted in any form or by any means, including photocopying, recording, or other electronic or mechanical methods, without the prior written permission of the publisher, except in the case of brief quotations embodied in critical reviews and certain other noncommercial uses permitted by copyright law. For permission requests, write to the publisher, addressed:

Connie Johnston
Train of Thought Press
2275 Huntington Drive, #306
San Marino, CA 91108
www.TrainOfThoughtPress.com

TRAIN OF THOUGHT
P R E S S

*"Injustice anywhere is a threat
to justice everywhere."
— Martin Luther King, Jr.
(Letter from a Birmingham Jail; April 16, 1963)*

This book is dedicated to my mom.
Thank you for the gift of unconditional love.

I first wrote these stories in early 2010, in cafes
across Israel and Egypt, but the 2016
Presidential election triggered the writing of
this final version.

This book is for the people who are unsatisfied
with our divisive culture.

CHAPTERS

PREFACE

"Put your bodies upon the gears."
— *Mario Savio*

The Old City of Jerusalem uniquely showcases a concept I refer to as the imprint of Zoe and Bios, an ancient Greek supposition of life which I believe may offer new meaning today to help us understand the effects of things like PTSD (post-traumatic stress disorder)

The Italian philosopher Giorgio Agamben asserted that there is a notable distinction between "bare life" (*zoe*) and "a particular mode of life" or "qualified life" (*bios*). I titled this book Zoe Bios because I believe we could benefit from an upgraded and simplified definition of these ancient and political terms to match our modern landscape.

I propose that Zoe is culture, Bios our living bodies, and DNA Memory is what holds and triggers our perceptions and behavior.

I believe each single human (and all) life is affected by both present-day and historical imprints, resulting in something I call DNA Memory: the familial health of our physical, emotional, intellectual, and spiritual selves.

Basically, my theory of DNA Memory is applied in this book and through real-life storytelling to explain the origins and energy of PTSD and its effects on people. But it must be said that this theory of DNA Memory—which is informed by the science of epigenetics—can explain much more.

One physical example: Randy Jirtle found in his breakthrough study that our genes are not fixed. He found two genetically identical mice looked vastly different—one was lean and brown, and the other was fat and yellow—after a controlled test. This is directly related to the food that was given to each mouse. In other words, what we consume or do not consume can leave tragic marks. It is proven that impoverished adolescents acquire DNA marks which lead to brain changes and cause depression. This is what epigenetic research tells us. And it's on to something bigger.

We are, as the old saying goes, the sum of our experiences. So, you can imagine that there are mental aspects to consider as well as physical, hence the need to look at Zoe, Bios, and DNA Memory.

In fact, the invisible wounds of our psyche can often do the most damage in terms of how we handle ourselves, our families, and our communities, let alone the idea of globalism and colonialism.

In this book, I take poetic license with the above concepts to present a fresh lens and possibly a new tool to help us understand the reasons why people perceive the world the way they do and maybe even help explain their behavior, too.

Here are some key questions for you to consider while reading these stories.

What if: Zoe is actively creating imprints into our DNA, and Bios is the energy utilizing the imprints, or what I call DNA Memory, that which influences our bodies and minds?

What if: DNA Memory is something so powerful that it influences the very lens through which each of us views the world, transcending (and yet responding to) cultural and immediate experiences. Zoe and Bios—presenting as DNA

Memory—impact the way we perceive everything from politics to religion, community, and family?

And what if, until we understand these primal influencers—which are woven into our individual and collective psyches—we cannot truly make the changes necessary for peace and harmony?

How does this relate to Jerusalem? You will see. I applied this new tool for understanding and found an interesting result. No matter who you are or what you believe (or do not believe), what is happening in the Middle East impacts all our lives in too many visible and invisible ways.

The city is riddled with visible imprints caused by Zoe—politics, religion, and never-ending war. It is a beautiful, yet battered multi-tiered cake. Every layer showcases yet another ruthless grab for power, each of which has caused lasting wounds, changing for the worse the city's Bios instincts and leaving lasting imprints on DNA Memory.

It is a beaten and bruised city that has changed hands a number of times. Impressively, in what could be called a miracle, it has somehow managed to keep its grace from each period. Unfortunately, this is not true for too many of its inhabitants who go about the business of repeating history, ever thickening our invisible scars.

I imagine siblings at the beach building sand structures. One brother designs beautiful churches and chapels, while the second constructs fantastic mosques with tall minarets, and the third labors over synagogues and temples, each certain that his creation is the finest. As the first child finishes his project and takes a step back to admire his kingdom, a brother rushes forward and knocks it down. The other brother, seizing the opportunity of distraction, does the same to the new victor, eager to build his righteous vision on top of the ruins. They repeat this cycle, building and destroying, repeatedly undermining one another's work, pausing only to state, "This is mine." All the while, they gloat at the distress of the others. They are proud brothers, each unable to accept victory unless it is his own.

It reminds me of how connected the United States—and much of Western society—is to the Middle East. Diasporas of all kinds were thrust into the cradle of civilization, drawn by its fertile land and sea, along with the trades and connections to far places.

Such is the never-ending conflict in the Middle East—the epic battleground of wills.

We've been conditioned to accept this as the status quo. We don't expect the conflict to be resolved anytime soon; no peace agreement is forthcoming. The repetitious news reports have dulled our senses, blunting the international community's capacity to care about the implications of this escalating war. We've lost our compassion for the citizens at the mercy of their leaders. If a car bomb were to explode in Times Square today, we'd be up in arms. We hear a similar news report from Syria and we change the channel. It's old news.

We seem blind to our own history. The United States has its own DNA Memory, shaped by slavery and oppression. We may be wise to advise Israel and the Palestinians that there is a better way forward, built on the pillars of respect for human rights and dignity—a path that steers clear of inhumane treatment.

It may be difficult to recognize these tenets in this new political moment—especially when systemic racism is still ruining the lives of people of color—but it is nonetheless true that we have more equity in the United States than ever before. Progress has been made since our original sin. As we reflect today, after the 25th anniversary of the '92 uprising in Los Angeles, we are reminded that we have much room for growth.

It is true we have earned new levels of equity and moral authority, but as Obama said in his farewell address, "All of us have more work to do." Our progress will begin to slip away if we don't keep pushing forward.

The tricky part is to see how the fear and hate we see in the United States today has largely been caused by foreign policy blunders of the past.

So, first, before we do anything else, we need to understand our imprints. Our current political landscape—considering what is happening in Syria, Iraq, Afghanistan, throughout the Middle East and, indeed, with Russia—is a direct result of decisions surrounding the birth of Israel in 1947, in which the United States had a vested interest.

That perilous decision made by Western powers is not the fault of the Israelis, and yet it is a burden that affects both Israelis and Palestinians alike.

Since our Western powers created this problem, it only makes sense that we, and our Eastern allies, should come to our brothers' and sisters' aid and figure out a way forward. The crux of this book is to ask us to consider that secular society is best abled to inspire and broker a peace deal, moreover, to improve our culture, and that energy toward this goal will improve the lives of the countless vulnerable communities in the world, simply by redirecting public funds away from the military and into public services. There are many benefits to this approach, but it's not as simple as a single decision or action.

Given the aforementioned, I offer the following lens as you read this book:

1. **Zoe**: Stories of real people in Israel and Egypt (collected less than a year before the Arab revolution) who are living a

tale different than the stories you read on the internet or see on TV;

2. **Bios**: How the imprints of our grandfathers and grandmothers, war, politics, our environment—not to mention luck—influence who we become; a paradigm shift in terms of how to view the stories of three monolithic religions and their 3,000+ year fight; and,

3. **DNA Memory**: A new way to understand people who differ from ourselves, to build our empathy muscle and empower us to make better decisions—from progressive policy-making to informed public fund allocation.

Perhaps you'll see, as I have, that the fibers of this family tree of faith instinctively sing a unified, peaceful song of hope. The leaders call for war, but the people call for peace.

Currently the peoples' song is stifled. We're lost in an ancient olive grove. Because the ache of each root clings tightly to its limited perspective, it cannot see the point of view of any other. Each gnarled branch emits a prerecorded cry, protesting pruning, even if the sacrifice of a limb would result in better health for all.

I propose that we clear a path and venture onto a mountaintop from which we can see the landscape in its entirety, for we must separate the whole from its strained individuals if we are to devise a way forward and leave better imprints on our DNA Memory, ones that serve to produce better instincts.

We're due for a hard pivot, and until it happens, the battles and status quo imprinting will continue. The will of the people—including their language and their culture, blinded by religion—will be painfully stuck in time. All of us will be stuck with a DNA Memory dominated by terrorism instead of peace.

That is what is happening to the Middle East, who have a bellyache because their ancestors gorged themselves on the rotted bark of war.

If you view this oldest of shining cities from the nearest hilltop, you will see that it is stunningly possessed. One of the most affecting visions of my adult life was the paradox of watching the kids play and families go about their day in a historical context soaked in conflict. With each breath and each movement, I could see the exchange of dark secrets between the people and the land. I, the agnostic visitor, witnessed the existence of ghosts from the past, lingering in the shadows. Can there be another place on earth that exudes this type of energy?

Who or what can imprint the minds and hearts of the young to go a different path? And in this populist political environment, defiled by trumped-up lies and gaslighting, whose perspective should we trust? Whose side should we take? Who owns what territory, and who is being terrorized?

For generations, Western power has waved capitalism and nationalism like a weapon. It's time to own up to the problem and find the right problem-solvers. We can no longer gobble up the world's resources and take advantage of disadvantaged people while benefiting the powerful few.

The moral high ground we try to portray to the world is smoke and mirrors unless our actions match our stated value system.

No doubt the wars in the Middle East have contributed to the avalanche of fear that has been changing political landscapes the world over. It is our responsibility to stop this madness.

All of this is easily linked to the Middle East and, of course, religion. The United States, a majority Christian country, is invested in its founding religion and the fate of Israel. To ignore these facts is akin to insisting that the world is flat.

American perception may begin and end between and within blue and red states, counties, and cities. We may remain uninformed, content to listen to the reverberations in our echo chamber. But we must ask ourselves: is living in a bubble making us safer? Who truly benefits from this isolation? Shouldn't we, after 9/11, know we're not immune to the conflicts rumbling across the ocean?

The current happenings in the Middle East and elsewhere impact all of us, and likely will impact us even more so in the future—if we don't make a hard pivot toward an energy of a new kind and intensity.

I don't pretend to have all the answers. However, I do have a theory to help us engage.

The award-winning BBC program *Naked Science* put forth the idea that every writer has a DNA of sorts. The premise is that even the best writers have a limited vocabulary, and therefore limited ability to express themselves. Capacity is unique and exclusive to each writer. Therefore, I have a set number of words with which to play, like a single-person Scrabble game.

As such, I can only share with you my perceptions and experience of this ancient battle between siblings. I offer a new lens with limited words, but possibly limitless applications.

I urge you to take matters into your own hands and vet any questions that arise. Test the theory yourself. Seek out facts and build your empathy muscle. Put the concepts of Zoe and Bios to work. Explore the idea of DNA Memory, then use this tool to help us move toward prosperity for all.

Our DNA Memory might be impacted by war, but peace is in the hearts and minds of mothers and fathers, young and old alike. It is easy to find that we share hope for and dreams of peace, equal opportunity, and a fair quality of life for all.

Most of all, I offer that DNA Memory is powerful in our present day. I believe that, in a single lifetime, we as individuals can change our trajectory as citizens in the world at large.

However, if enough of us make this shift and begin to perceive the world through a clearer lens, we can set a new tone that positively impacts our local and global culture for generations to come.

CHAPTER 1 – Our Journey

"It's never too late to be what you might have been."
— George Elliot

My introduction to Jerusalem was perfectly timed; I first arrived in this fair city during a lovely winter sunset at a time of peace. I did not view the West Bank that day, although I did pass one of the much-disputed security walls while traveling down the highway.

The winding road teased me with a lovely view as we approached.

In the distance, I got a glimpse of the Old City. I saw new development, tall cranes like gigantic African birds frozen in place. I perceived something heavy as we got closer, but wasn't sure at that time whether it was my anticipation or something else. I sensed that the peaceful atmosphere obscured the truth.

I was impressed by this modern city as we approached the bus station. A helpful young Jewish architect working at the Bauhaus Museum in Tel Aviv told me about the influx of

German-Jewish architects in Palestine after the rise of the Nazis. They fled their European homes before the Holocaust was fully underway, and once in Palestine, these men designed the prevailing unifying aesthetic of the '30s housing boom. This metropolitan "white city" is now recognized by UNESCO as a World Heritage Site for having the largest concentration of modernist-style buildings in the world.

There is impressive architecture around the city, although much of it is in disrepair. Tel Aviv is similar to Jerusalem in that war has left its mark. Once upon a time, the open-style architecture of Tel Aviv flowed with its natural landscape, but the beauty of the city is now overshadowed by a devastated psyche. The people of this great city are affected and anxious. Both architecture and people alike have been visibly affected by the years of conflict.

I was struck by the dirty tears of the once-beautiful landmark buildings falling from shuttered windows, the perpetual stains dripping down their cheeks. Ancient air-conditioning units and crackled paint mar the façade like age-spots and scars haphazardly scattered across its skin. Apartment homes, rising stories above the busy streets, showed signs of life, and I was led to wonder: of what quality was that life?

Millions live in the same sad buildings, each just like the other. All of them battered and bruised. None spared.

Along the beautiful Mediterranean beach, I saw new oceanfront homes under construction, built by and for millionaires. In the bowels of the city, I saw evidence of more new growth as well, and while some of it was quite cutting-edge, my overall impression was infused with crowded lanes, traffic jams, and car horns blaring non-stop to the beat of a clanging drum, overlapping the typical sounds you'd hear in any big city. The sounds of heavy equipment competed with the sounds of people rushing to get wherever they needed to go in their dented cars or sooty scooters, slipping through traffic and sometimes even driving on the sidewalks— taking all available routes to push ahead.

As I walked the streets, it was difficult to overlook the past and harder still to ignore the present situation. The family saga and ongoing storyline are obvious. Like a junkie's arm, the evidence is unmistakable: the sickness of war lives there.

As I rode the public bus from Jerusalem to Tel Aviv, the people's urgency struck me. We had barely stopped at the station when riders began rushing, bumping into each other as they evacuated the bus. I'd often seen people anxious to get on and off the subway during NYC rush hour back in the States, but the need to get off this bus was stronger than anything I'd experienced in Berlin or elsewhere, as if there were something serious at stake. It was a race to the door.

Alert faces and heavy energy filled the space. Everyone moved briskly, regardless of age, each determined to exit. Patience was limited; accidental delays were immediately addressed with words to keep moving.

What lives inside the Jewish DNA Memory?

Most of us understand that environmental concerns are not on the minds of people in third-world countries because they are too busy struggling to survive to worry about the proper disposal of trash and prevention of pollution. Likewise, Israelites—who, for the most part, do not live in a third-world environment but do live with pressures and limitations that have shaped who they are as a people—are also desperately trying to survive.

The family that hosted me was an exception. They were a connected and caring team of individuals. Their home was my home base in Tel Aviv.

But like all countries and peoples, every culture has its own flavor, and I quickly discovered that Israel presents a harsh instinct, or dare I say, DNA Memory imprint.

It's interesting and terribly sad to see where the oppression of the Jews has taken them. Israel's path, complete with the continued conflict with the Palestinians, has been a painful journey.

Since the beginning of history, the Jewish people have been kicked out of their homeland and thrust into diaspora. They were forced to find new means of survival and were encouraged to use brains over brawn and to provide for their own human dignity.

More than people who owned and worked land and participated in the development of early industry, or uncomplicated people who lived a nomadic or sedentary tribal life, the Jews had to use their minds to survive. They became superb thinkers—and survivors.

The following are some of the several factors that influenced Jewish cultural advancement:

1. Early and broad adoption of reading and writing within their cultural community;

2. Their religion asked for conscious coupling of skilled and intelligent people; and,

3. The forced diaspora of the Jewish people, resulting in access to the best practices from around the world, but most specifically from Europe.

As a result, Jewish culture benefited greatly from various industrial developments and modern enlightenments.

Charles Murray of the American Enterprise Institute and author of *The Bell Curve,* a controversial book about the IQ levels of different peoples, instigated a stormy discussion in 1994 that factors into this conversation.

Murray postures plainly that genetics determine IQ, arguing for nature versus nurture or environment. Many thought his was a racist approach. He overlooked a critical factor—the matter of evolution, the reasons why and ways people evolve. He chose to focus instead on the "superiority" of one group over another.

I think he's patently wrong in his view.

It's not as simple as saying one group is better than another. We must understand what has shaped us and why. And because we are equal as humans, it's even more important to recognize that each of us is equally capable if given the opportunity.

Is it luck or something else? I believe it is indeed how we are nurtured and the environment in which we live that shapes us— primarily, our time in history, geography, things learned/observed/felt/expressed/experienced, events, family, love, sex, fears, and culture. These are the things that cause genetic changes and are the product of evolution and DNA Memory.

With respect, we may think of DNA Memory as a poetic interpretation of epigenetics, an ever-emerging science seemingly proving that what we call nurturing (or lack thereof) is what makes nature.

Imagine all the lives that were lived up to yours. The memories of your parents, grandparents, great-grandparents, and even great-great-grandparents live in your DNA, shaping who you are today.

It's another way to explain instinct.

Charles Murray called Jewish and white people "superior," but I think his idea doesn't take into account the big picture. It's clear specific groups of people have advanced in the modern world more than others, but the words "advanced" and "superior" have distinctly different meanings.

One way of thinking states explicitly that one group of people or a person is better than another, end of story. The concept of DNA Memory offers that we're all equal, but each of us have been shaped by the particular environmental factors to which we (and our ancestors) were exposed. It proposes that dramatic evolution is possible even within one lifetime, with credit given to both experiences we have and the experiences of those before us. Of course, we can't discount luck, either.

I propose that DNA Memory produces the attributes of specific groups of people, and that DNA Memory is alive and being shaped as I write and you read.

Our DNA Memory matters, but what matters more is the next step—understanding why.

CHAPTER 2 – Common Ground

"We have to find ways of organizing ourselves with the rest of humanity. It has to be everybody or nobody."
— Buckminster Fuller

After spending three weeks in Tel Aviv, I took the 45-minute bus ride to Jerusalem, the contested capital of Israel and of what has been historically called Palestine.

The Old City is the true center of Jerusalem. It defines Israel as a whole and is the central battleground between the Jews and Muslims.

Once inside the station, I walked past shops and American fast food outlets alongside mom-and-pop shops selling shawarma. Some of the shops sold luxuries while others peddled old market items like locally made blankets and jewelry.

At each entrance and exit, Israeli army kids were posted. I call them "kids" because they were in fact quite young (usually between 18-20). They posed with smiles in the way only the young do, although in their case, they did so with an air that made me think they were under too much pressure.

They were dressed in plain, all-green uniforms. Their pants hung low and were stuffed into their belts. They wore tall, black steel-toed boots and shouldered their M16 rifles, watching me closely as I passed by.

I certainly stood out from the rest of the mob, but they saw I was innocent enough and eventually let me be. I suspect they were curious because I was alone and didn't arrive on a tour bus. Instead, I rode in on a public bus full of locals, direct from Tel Aviv.

It took me a little while to find the correct exit, but eventually I got past security and left the bus station. I found the taxi line and was dropped off at a hostel about 10 minutes away where I stored my bag.

I hit the streets—the main part of the Midrachov, Ben Yehuda Street. I saw Hasidic Jews rapping on the corner selling albums. Tourists and locals alike were out enjoying the evening, buying this or that, having dinner, or meeting friends for drinks. I was eavesdropping when some Jews from Brazil said that they thought Americans were stupid, although I only overheard the end of the conversation. I went to bed early but was kept up late by a dance club that was open past four in the morning— again, Hasidic Jews having a good time.

I was eager to explore when the sunlight finally crept over the horizon and into my window. I jumped out of bed and made my way.

Walking up to the Old City made me feel small and keenly alive, like a character in Voltaire's *Micromégas*. I was a new micro-element in the ancient ecosystem.

I entered the Old City through a small entryway. A temporary fence had been erected due to construction, forcing people from all corners of the world to line up and wait together. As soon as we got through the entryway, we split; the tourists and groups were quick to follow guides to their scheduled tours. They explored the quadrants of the Old City: the Jewish Quarter, the Christian Quarter, the Armenian Quarter, and the Muslim Quarter. I watched this for a moment, relishing my freedom, and decided to take my own path, not following any particular person or group.

My plan was to visit the Western Wall first, but I approached this labyrinth of a city like the rest of my journey, following my gut.

I got lost, which is very easy to do in the Old City. As soon as I realized I did not know where I was, a friendly man recognized my confusion and asked me where I wanted to go. To make it easy on him, and to give myself a focal point on the map, I told him I was looking for the Western Wall, and he pointed me in the right direction. I thanked him and continued to walk.

People of all ages were outside enjoying the day. It rarely rains in Israel. Like California's drought, it rains only a few weeks a year, if they're lucky. It was lovely outside. Warm, with blue skies dotted by a few cumulus clouds— scattered bright white puffs changing shapes and seemingly moving in the same direction as I was.

Young boys played with a soccer ball within a semi-enclosed area, surrounded by stout white rock walls overlooking the Mount of Olives.

A twenty-something couple snuggled up on a similar barrier wall were reading to each other but stopped to look up at me as I approached. I passed a two-story religious school with a large courtyard in front, which was either letting out for a break or starting. I didn't see many tourists, but it started to get crowded.

Teachers led a group of small children who looked happy. They had a distinctive energy about them that set them apart from the American children I usually saw back home. They shared something that radiated from inside them like a weight pushing through the air, or perhaps like the scent of a looming storm.

It seemed to me that the old men working the various trade shops have felt this weight for too long. It showed on their faces, like gravity was heavier for them here. I didn't see many older women, but did see young women, many of them soldiers.

I asked for directions again, to make sure I was on the right path. I gave it a try in Hebrew, but the young couple helped me in English.

Most people in Israel speak English, the universal language. For this, I was very lucky and grateful. They told me I was going the right way, so I continued down the hill and ended up in a tight corridor, surrounded by tall, menacing walls.

I had obviously veered off-path and hit a dead end. A young Arab man who was alone crafting something with his hands sat on a raggedy chair some meters away. He was the only person within sight, so I approached him. Just as our eyes met and I opened my mouth to ask for directions, another man—an Englishman, coming out of what seemed like nowhere—cut me off.

He gave me a look and pointed to something behind me, opposite of the Arab seated before me. I spun around to find a handmade sign pointing to a much smaller, darker corridor. It read, "This way to the Western Wall."

I turned back to find the mysterious man had turned and was now walking up the hill. The young Arab man, who was staring at me, acknowledged the odd exchange with a smirk and nodded for me to follow the sign.

I later found out that this was an informal entrance, used by locals. I apparently missed the road that tourists take, on the complete opposite side, near the parking lot.

CHAPTER 2 – Common Ground

I made my way through the tight path and ended up at a security checkpoint. The guards looked me up and down as if to say, "Who are you to come this way, and alone?" but they thoughtfully directed me through the process. The security was high, much like that of airports. I (and my belongings) had to pass through an x-ray to check for weapons.

With a reserved smile and minimal eye contact, I passed through the checkpoint, retrieved my things, and entered the wide-open space.

I'd made it to the Western Wall. I took my time walking down the slope to get as close as I could. I found a plaque that provided written context of the sacred site in both Hebrew and English. Interestingly, it framed the Biblical scripture, "My house is a house of prayer for all peoples" (Isaiah 56:7).

Sadly, it is not truly for all peoples. Muslims are not allowed to share this site.

The Jews believe this wall, before which they rock, pray, and wail, is the earthly place at which they can get closest to the beginnings of the world, where God took the ashes from the land and made Adam. It has become a place of pilgrimage for Jews, as many view it as the closest permitted accessible site to the holiest spot in Judaism, namely the Foundation Stone, which lies on the Temple Mount. It is said this is where Abraham prepared his son Isaac for sacrifice. A majority of Jewish religious commentators propose that this was the place where God tested Abraham to see if he would actually kill his own son, as a test of his loyalty.

Much has happened here.

The Temple Mount, the area above the Western Wall, is the location of the Dome of the Rock. It is not a mosque. Rather, it is a shrine built to showcase the glory of Islam in hope that the monotheistic religions will unite.

The Foundation Stone, also called "the Rock," is underneath the dome and although is considered one of the holiest spots for Jews, it is also believed that this is the site of the Holy of Holies—both Solomon's Temple and Herod's Temple. This area is also restricted. Jews are not allowed in for a few reasons, but mostly because Muslims believe this was the ultimate destination for Muhammad—the spot where he ascended on his night journey with his horse into the heavens.

They believe it is theirs alone, a sacred spot for Muslims.

This is the real ground zero.

No authority asked for proof of my religious affiliation. Maybe some level of profiling protected me because I look neither Jewish nor Muslim. Or maybe they aren't strict about enforcing the rules. It was harder for me to get into the Dome of the Rock than the Western Wall; before they granted me access, I was questioned as to where I came from and what I was doing there.

While I was still at the Western Wall, I made my way to the only side I was allowed to access, because of course, this too was segregated—men to the left and women to the right. I took a seat, closed my eyes, and offered up one of the most earnest prayers of my life. I figured, why not? No harm. No foul. Remaining true to my beliefs, I uttered an agnostic prayer of peace for all cultures and creeds.

About twenty minutes later, I took my prayer—written on a small, tightly rolled-up piece of paper—and added it to the wall like millions before me had already done. Maybe it is still stuck between two stones alongside countless other notes and personal prayers from people around the world. Apparently, the Jewish authorities collect the prayers twice a year and bury them on the nearby Mount of Olives. None are thrown away.

At this point I wanted to go up and see the Dome of the Rock, but I wanted to find it myself with no map in hand, so I decided to exit the way I entered and search for a different entrance.

I walked back up the hill and turned right—a new direction—which took me directly into the Muslim Quarter, though at the time I didn't realize where I was. I walked through markets where merchants sold everything under the sun (or rather, in the shade). There was no roof because it was an open market, but the walls were so high at points that they blocked much of the sun. The paved streets were covered with stones worn smooth from the foot traffic of countless generations.

The stones reminded me of another ancient locality—possibly the oldest port in the world—located in Jaffa, Tel Aviv.

Architecture is not only beautiful, but it has a voice, and it tattles. The stories and history of a place are told through materials and craftsmanship. The vision and execution are open for all to see. Stones lay on top of stones across pathways, walls, and ceilings. Everything about its construction felt sturdy, the colors and textures telling stories of the past.

The history of the Old City is alive and well. I was walking briskly, trusting my gut to take me where I needed to go, when I turned another corner and came across an older man with open, honest blue eyes. He made direct eye contact and approached me, coming almost too close as he asked me where I wanted to go. I usually take the time to chat with locals—in fact, it's a priority for me when I travel—but I answered without slowing down. I saw a bright light at the end of a dark corridor, and without hesitating I said, "This way, thank you." I turned into the dark alley, leaving the man to repeat his question to my backside as I walked away.

I felt as though I had seen a vision, and I followed it, not knowing why I was compelled to do so, but obeying my instincts nonetheless.

I picked up the pace as I passed more merchant offerings. I was on a mission. Another man, this time in his twenties, walked out of his shop and matched my pace as he called out to me, "You can't go this way."

Again, I didn't stop. For some reason, I chose not to listen to him, either. I politely said, "I want to see for myself, thank you." To which he replied, "Okay. When you figure it out, come back and have tea with me." I gave him a quick smile and, starting to wonder if I should have listened to the older man, said, "Okay."

I finally slowed down as I started up the stairs, not knowing what was behind that poltergeist-like light that drew me in. Suddenly two soldiers with rifles ready commanded me to stop. I continued forward, but they shouted, "Stop! You cannot enter here!" At this point, I finally came out of my trance and stopped to face them. They said in unison, "You need to go back to the Western entrance. This is for Muslims only."

CHAPTER 2 – Common Ground

Apparently, I walked straight up to the holiest entrance for Muslims into the Temple Mount. Another local secret entrance.

Finally, I understood the fuss. I offered a respectful apology, and the soldiers chatted with me for a while, then gave me proper directions.

The exchange ended cordially, so I turned around to share some tea with my new friend, the young man.

He chuckled when I approached his shop. I smiled and shrugged, saying, "I had to see for myself," as I winked. He laughed louder this time and, with a bright smile, asked, "Do you like sugar in your tea?" I told him that I didn't, and with that he sat me down and disappeared for a few minutes. This gave me a moment to observe his shop. It was the size of a large walk-in closet in an upscale American home. He had mostly touristy goods—porcelain Old City replicas in various sizes and lovely blankets—but nothing original, and certainly not enough of a selection to compete with the stores around him. It looked to me like he was just getting started.

When he returned with my tea, we went through the usual question-and-answer series—where was I from, what was I doing, how old was I, why was I doing this, where was I staying, for how long, what was next, and so on. I asked him many of the same questions, some of which were delicate topics. These were questions about his faith, such as how he practices his religion and his interpretations of Jihad. I admitted to him that I'd only met or had significant friendships with a few Muslims, and I was very curious, open, and agnostic. The latter made him curious as well. He was surprised that I would want to come to Jerusalem even though I'm not religious.

To cut to the point, he said he wanted nothing to do with a religious war. He wanted to live a life like any other twenty-something kid. He liked to dance. He liked girls. He had dreams, like the rest of us. His big vision was to turn his little shop, with the help of his father, into a profitable business. He didn't want to work for somebody else.

Sounds like the American dream to me.

We enjoyed our time together, learning a few things about our different cultures, and then I took my leave. All that walking made me hungry. He had to stay and manage the shop, and I had to continue my journey.

We exchanged info and I went on my way, finding myself a bit lost again, but it all worked out because three young boys offered to help me find "the best hummus in the world." They joked and laughed the entire time we walked back up the hill, taking me through the maze on a path I certainly would not have found on my own—a shortcut, or the scenic route. I let them have the glory of thinking they hustled the lost American and gave each of them 10 shekels once we got to our destination.

As I waited for my food, I reviewed the day thus far—the men and women at the Western Wall, the locals, the interesting groups of religious tourists from countless denominations, my chat with the young man. For some unknown reason, I couldn't get the older man's bright blue eyes out of my head. He was a peaceful creature. He wanted to help me, but I plowed past him, undeterred from my path. I deliberately ignored him. What very strange behavior that was—so unlike me. Why did I do that?

The food came just in time. Distracted from my thoughts, I focused on satisfying my hearty appetite and ate some of the best food in the world.

Eager to get back on my trek, I made my way through the maze of the Old City to get to the Temple Mount. I had to go again through the security gate that I accidentally found earlier, the only way I knew to get to my destination.

The Western entrance, the one I was supposed to take the first time, is also the entrance to the Temple of the Dome. I entered through the local side and exited on the Western side to get to the Temple of the Mount entrance. It was a bit confusing to navigate.

The Temple Mount was closed for Muslim prayer, so I got in line with more than 50 people and waited for the new security gate to open up and let us in.

The line kept growing, and soon the area was crowded with people. I wasn't the only one in line to find it unnerving that troops of Israeli soldiers began to line up, hundreds of them moving together toward the Jewish monument, passing by our line. They carried huge personal bags, walking in small cliques, again smiling and laughing. They looked more like summer camp participants than a new generation of soldiers.

I don't see any other nation educating and training their young like Israel. They find the best and make them better, placing top people in relevant positions of power both while in the military and after service to the state, in civilian life. This makes for an efficient and obviously effective system, one of which most of the citizens are proud. More impressively, the kids themselves are proud, in an almost snobbish way.

Finally, the line started to move. We walked across creaking planks of wood, which felt like a long temporary bridge, navigating our way through complicated ropes and blockades.

A very different entrance than the Western Wall.

Once through the last leg of the herd mechanism, we were received by another line of armed Jordanian soldiers before being granted entrance.

I was trying to soak it all in when I heard a voice say to me, "Are you going to pass me again?" Sure enough, the older man I had so rudely passed earlier was standing to my left and behind me. I immediately greeted him, saying, "Nice to see you again." He told me he had come there to wait for me.

This is how our friendship began. He told me that he felt it was important for him to show me around the Old City. Then he expressed his wish for peace, to end the war between the Arabs and the Jews. All this before we even exchanged names.

He stated his message frankly, expressing his desire that I listen to what he had to say because he had an important message of peace that he felt I needed to hear. I wasn't sure what to think of his forthright manner or assertiveness, but felt it was worth my time to have a local show me around.

He told me he was born and raised in the Old City, where he continues to live with extended family as the head of a very large household. His people were originally from Iran but have lived in Palestine for thousands of years. He explained that this is how he looks at it, from an ancient timeline.

Still this is all modern compared to how historians view the ancient people of Judea.

He had worked as a guide for twenty of his fifty-something years. We spent the next couple of days together.

First, he walked me around the Temple Mount, explaining the history of each gate and sharing what he believed was the perspective of each religion. He briefly went over the history of the Ottoman Empire and the last development of the Old City, explaining what we see today and the layer upon layer of development that is hidden beneath what is currently visible.

He pointed out that the Golden Gate has special meaning. This entrance is for the next Jewish Messiah, or the return of Jesus. Muslims put their graves there to block that entrance and sealed off the gate precisely for the purpose of preventing any so-called Jewish Messiah from returning. Jews won't walk on graves, so the thought is that the placement of the graves, combined with the sealing of the gate, will prevent the next Jewish Messiah from returning there.

To what extremes these two brothers fight each other! It made my new friend shake his head.

After I told him that I needed to take some time to "meditate" and that I wanted to give the same prayer here as I did at the Western Wall, he took me to his personal or secret spot. We walked toward the Golden Gate and sat down on a short wall.

He pointed out that we were aligned with the church behind me, the mosque in front of us, and the temple beyond that. This was his prayer spot.

We both sat in silence for about 20 minutes, or until we were forced to leave the Temple Mount as it was to close again. All non-Muslims were quickly ushered out.

After we left the Temple Mount, we went to get a better view of the city from atop the Lutheran church tower. My guide delivered a dizzying diatribe about the development of various points of interests and the various beliefs associated with each monument, such as the Church of the Holy Sepulchre, which the final stop for the crucified Jesus after his purported Via Dolorosa ("Way of Grief" or "Way of Suffering") down the winding hillside into the Old City. He took me to the most holy place for countless Christian denominations.

The steps up were exhausting. As we walked back down them, my chat with the young Muslim man lingered in my mind.

Since I was ready for a rest and a snack, the older man took me to get authentic Arab food. He also suggested that we pick up a delicious dessert called akanfe, made of honey and cheese, at one of his favorite local spots.

It was there, surrounded by local Muslims, that I asked him the same questions I had asked the young man over tea.

His responses were similar to the young man's, although he was more optimistic. He said he believed that peace was possible, that there was a way to find peace through understanding and acceptance, and that we must share natural resources, land, and economies.

He used a biblical explanation to help me comprehend the misunderstanding between these two distant brothers in order to show

how this animosity goes all the way back to Abraham.

The Jews are descendants of Abraham's son Isaac.

The Arabs are descendants of Abraham's son Ishmael.

Because Ishmael was the son of a slave woman (Genesis 16:1-16) and Isaac was the promised son who would inherit the blessings of Abraham (Genesis 21:1-3), obviously, there was inherent animosity between the two sons. The situation was set up for conflict from the very beginning, since the two sons had different birthrights.

After Ishmael mocked Isaac (Genesis 21:9), Sarah talked Abraham into sending Hagar and Ishmael away (Genesis 21:11-21).

This likely caused even more contempt in Ishmael's heart toward Isaac. This is especially important to consider if you take this story as a historical retelling and the beginnings of setting DNA Memory.

CHAPTER 2 – Common Ground

My guide said, "It is devastating, what has happened, but does not have to be fatalistic for Jerusalem, or the world at large."

He said that everyday people want peace. They are sick of the fight and want to find a new way forward. "It's the fault of the politicians and so-called leaders that there is this continued war," he said.

He gave me hope. As did, I should mention, my conversations with friends in Tel Aviv. It's important for me to note one such conversation that I had with a veteran of the Second Lebanese War.

Instead of distrusting and disliking Muslims—which could be easy to do because of his experience—this veteran was working to convince his friends that it was in the best interests of the Jews and of Israel to befriend and improve the quality of life available to neighboring Muslims. He shared beautiful stories of growing up on a kibbutz with a mother who taught music as a form of art therapy for Muslim children. His father was a farmer who shared his knowledge with neighboring Muslim villages. This twenty-something young man had a vision, something unique to offer the world at large—a Marshall Plan of sorts for the Middle East.

As I sat in the café with my guide, the Muslim peace activist, it felt like hanging out with an old friend. It was a blessing that made both of us happy as we decided to continue my exploration with a trip to the Mount of Olives. However, my happy feelings dissipated as the bright sun revealed a sad reality which hit me deep in my gut.

East Jerusalem and the Muslim neighborhoods were depressing to walk through. There is a radical difference between even the worst Jewish neighborhoods and Muslim territories that look more like—or could even be called—a third-world living environment, not quite developing communities.

Dirty, unmaintained street corners overflowed with trash. Large, painted wood or slightly modern but still archaic signs were propped up in front of shoddy shops. Young kids in dirty clothes and in desperate need of showers played in the streets alongside broken-down cars.

The homes looked patched together, many of them made up of exposed rebar with open roofs. These unfinished homes spoke of promises made that people were unable to keep—homes waiting for future generations to revive their dreams.

Food was made and sold on broken curbsides. When I made eye contact with the kids in this part of town, I saw curiosity but also distrust in their eyes. The young men and women of the area seemed even more jaded than the children. A glint of hatred gleamed in their suspicious glances.

It was obvious that life in the Muslim area was much more difficult than on Ben Yehuda Street, where I hung out the previous night in the modern part of Jerusalem. That section of town is controlled by the Jews, and while it has suffered its share of terrorist attacks, it was flowing freely with a wide variety of commerce in clean, well-maintained shops. Tourists and locals walked the streets freely, smiling and enjoying themselves.

Life may be heavy for the Israeli citizens, but I realized that it is lighter than it is for Palestinians.

The struggles of East Jerusalem are reflected by the buildings, streets, and people. These starkly different (if not difficult) living conditions are literally blocks away from brand new Jewish malls and luxury housing. These areas are adjacent to one another because Israel has decided to move into some Palestinian areas, expanding development.

Israel's glittering expanse leers menacingly closer to the Palestinians living next door.

We made our way to East Jerusalem by taking a bus up the winding hill. Then we walked through a small section on our way to the Church of Pastor Naster, the place where it is said Jesus first recited the Lord's Prayer, which is offered in 62 different languages. This means that tourists around the world must go through this contested territory, the area where the Palestinians want to create their own capital—right alongside Israel—and to get to major monuments.

This would be fine—if only it were safe. Sadly, East Jerusalem is a war zone—not quite like the West Bank or Gaza, but the likes of a war zone nonetheless—so I was grateful my friend was with me as we passed through.

This time a Catholic nun sought me out. I reluctantly stopped and took the time to answer her questions. My answers made her happy. She was from my region: Southern California.

She was thin, short, and humped over, but she looked strong. Her Catholic dress and head coverings were spotless.

When we finished the basics of getting to know each other, we looked deeply into each other's eyes and didn't speak for a moment as our smiles grew. It was marvelous.

We seemed to make some sort of unexpected connection. I still don't know why she took to me, as my guide had, but I know why I liked her.

Much like him, she was all love and smiles. She was quick to take our minds off the heart-rending reality surrounding us and into the world of her religion, which was her sanctuary. Without any sort of announcement, she started showing us around. She broke from all the tourists and gave us a personal tour of her special place.

My guide was stunned. He told me, "She's always welcoming, but I've never seen her do that."

Our last moment matched the continued serendipitous happenings of my DNA Memory trek overall and of my journey around the Old City.

After we ate dinner, when I ordered tea, he interrupted me by saying, "No sugar, right?" to which I replied, "Yes, how did you know that?"

He finished our order before he would answer, then said that he had followed me the day I walked up to the blinding light of the Muslim entrance to the Temple Mount. I hadn't seen him there, but he said he stayed close by to make sure I would be all right.

And when I entered the young man's shop, he—my future guide—was the person, out of my sight, who prepared my tea and asked the young man to welcome me. He said the young man was surprised, as they know each other and this was obviously odd behavior for a guide—not to buy and make tea for a stranger, but to then not introduce himself.

In other words, this older man was taking care of me before we exchanged names, before we became friends, and before knowing anything about me, wanting nothing in return. (I did pay him for his time, but he refused to accept his normal day rate.) We both had felt a connection before we truly met. I asked him why he was so kind to a stranger. He said, "I had a feeling. I wanted to be your friend."

His statement seemed symbolic and meaningful. Was he just a guy looking to make a buck on a lost tourist? Or did he sense that I would listen to his story and seek to understand what was happening to his people? Did he have a feeling that I was a different kind of seeker in the Holy City? That I could tell its story?

Agreement is not needed to have a respectful conversation. The connection we made by listening to each other deserves respect at minimum.

CHAPTER 3 – Perspective

"Friends show their love in times of trouble, not in happiness." —Euripides

My guide and new friend wasn't the only Muslim or Palestinian I got to know while in the Middle East. I was honored to make connections and have meaningful discussions with half a dozen people across Israel and Egypt.

A month after my trip to Jerusalem, I traveled to Egypt in pursuit of a deeper understanding of Israel's relationship with its neighbor. I wanted to get a broader Muslim perspective of what was happening between Israel and the Palestinians.

I traveled from the Sinai Desert and across the Red Sea (the same sea that the original migrating tribes from Africa crossed, expanding from there into the human race around the world). Then I made my way up to Cairo, and farther north to Alexandria, the beautiful Mediterranean city infamous for its ancient and, more recently, renovated library—a city library still shaping minds and inspiring a sense of hope for people around the world.

It was a valuable experience. Egypt's history and landmarks, like in the nation of Israel, exposed current affairs. Months later, the Arab Revolution would erupt.

With sadness, I observed that modern Cairo—and, to a large extent, Egypt's overall heyday—was on its way out. There was a dark shadow looming over the city, growing darker as past glories began to say goodnight. All I could do at the time was hope Cairo would see another—even brighter and clearer—day of glory in the future.

When you drive into Cairo, you enter a black and white world. All color is lost in the thick pollution clogging the air (offering possibly the worst air quality in the region). It soon chokes your lungs and deposits a dirty film upon just about everything. Hair, skin, buildings, and possessions—everything shows decades of layers. Litter clutters the streets, coupled with unemployed and disadvantaged persons. The upper percent was nowhere to be found outside television and corruption.

At the time, I remembered that a few years earlier Ayman Nour—one of Egypt's most prominent political dissidents and a one-time presidential candidate—was unexpectedly released from prison after the United States and European governments had pressed for years to have him set free. Mr. Nour's imprisonment ended Egypt's brief experiment with opposition politics. His Al Gahd Party was the only legal opposition; it had a thriving anti-establishment following. In 2005, Mr. Nour garnered 600,000 votes in his bid for the presidency, placing a distant second behind Mr. Mubarak in a race controlled by the president's governing party.

As I explored Egypt, I repeatedly asked myself, "Where are the dissident voices of today?" They were nowhere to be found.

I asked a taxi driver to give me some examples of what President Mubarak had accomplished for his country, how the leadership was working to improve the living conditions and offer more opportunity. The driver looked at me squarely in the rear-view mirror and put his hand over his mouth, insinuating it wasn't acceptable for him to speak his mind.
Enough said, or, well… you get the point.

Another key thing to note is that Egypt bitterly opposed the UN partition of Palestine in 1948 and played an important role in the Arab-Israeli Wars that followed. Even though Egypt has ratified an armistice with Israel, relations between the two countries continue to be tense.

This relationship is critical, which is why the United States and President Barack Obama leveraged Cairo as the location for an important speech on and directed to the Muslim world.

During this speech, Obama highlighted human rights, taking aim at terrorist organizations that do not represent the majority of Muslims and pledging friendship with peaceful Arab and Muslim nations and communities.

And though I don't think he lived up to the brilliantly orated rhetoric, I believe he was saying the right things and sending the right signals.

"Mutual interests" and "respect" were his central points.

He spoke about the role ancient Islam played in educating Europe and its role in the enviable enlightenments—how the philosophies of the Arab world made up the foundational bedrock of modern academics and scholarship in the Western world.

In the history of the world, no cultural or linguistic group looms larger than Semitic peoples. Originating from the Arabian Peninsula, the Semitic people are responsible for the first civilizations, three major world religions, and a set of cultural practices that have been globalized or universalized more than any other peoples, including the Chinese and Europeans.

Therefore, my journey into Egypt was needed, and made for some interesting conversations in what is assuredly a modern and moderate— yes, I'll repeat, a moderate—Muslim country.

And I'll preface the following discussions with the fact that the people I met spoke English and, no doubt, all had a level of education that made a huge difference in how those particular people related to me, the United States, the West as a whole and, likely, to Israel.

I'm not ignorant to this important fact. If I had hired an interpreter who could help me interview locals in their native Arabic, I might have to share a much different story.

There is an optimistic way to look at this. English as a universal language has advantages. There are numerous benefits to having a cultural language (such as Hebrew and Arabic) and a universal language (such as English).

From Egyptian service workers and locals on a bus ride to Cairo, to a young man who recently completed his master's degree in Middle Eastern Studies and a manager at one of the finest and oldest hotels in all of Egypt—they told me the same thing.

These people were surprisingly consistent in their message.

Those with little education believe everything in the Qur'an and what their leaders tell them is "truth." Those with more education and curious minds believe the overall philosophy behind the Qur'an to deliver "truth" in the context of a broader message.

About 50 percent of the Muslim men told me they interpret Jihad as a holy war, which was to be waged against all non-believers, but again, this view was split along education levels.

All of them asserted, "We do not want war."

The more educated the person, the more likely they were to say they believed that Jihad can have a more peaceful, personal meaning. So... maybe you're realizing something as you read this, just as I did when I interviewed these people.

Education is critical to peace. Language is critical to education.

The Muslim men I spoke to unanimously said that more than anything else, Islam is a culture of good people, and that the radical fundamentalists did not represent them.

The flipside of the story is that Jews are not well-liked by Muslims. In fact, they are quite misunderstood and, frankly, sometimes hated.

It's not a surprise, though very interesting, that the response to my question, "What is your opinion about Israel?" reliably elicited a primal and quickly delivered response. Without much thought, each man said something to the effect of, "What they are doing to the Palestinians makes me sick to my stomach. If I lived there, I would kill them."

Let's think about this for a moment and go back to our survival spectrum. Like the Jews rudely rushing and pushing off the bus, doing whatever it takes to get ahead with all their skill, these Arab Muslim men have their own ideas of what is right and wrong. Their attitude is more extreme, shaped over time because of vastly different factors and variables.

I don't know anyone who doesn't experience aching empathy when they see oppressed people. The results of war are horrific. We see how hopeless Syria has become.

The reaction by Muslims to what is happening in Israel is beyond visceral. It hits them like only horrifying fear can. Their reactions are grounded in pure survival instinct. Their DNA Memory is revealed as they answer my questions.

The fearful reactions I observed in Muslims made me think about the wolf in a Jack London book, *White Fang*, translated into human behavior, an evolution absurdly harsh that resulted in heroic character. It's a fantastic fictional story that, for me, paints the picture of DNA Memory very well. We can and do recover from oppression and fear and learn how to function well in society and the world at large, as a result of (and not in spite of) the difficulties we face.

Let's look at the details affecting the Palestinians—a story all too familiar to many Arabs. A rebellion against colonialism may have more to do with our current state of affairs than that of Islam.

The British occupied the land of Palestine after the fall of the Ottoman Empire and before handing the rights over to Israel. To rephrase that, Western power colonized Palestine for many decades before making a decision to give it back, and when they relinquished their rights to the land, they did not give it back to the Palestinians. They gave it to the Jewish people.

"A number of scholars have pointed out that the revolutionary discourse of many modern Muslim leaders has most in common with the ideologies of resistance employed by Third

World national liberation and self-determination movements," wrote Khaled Abou El Fadl, currently Professor of Law at UCLA. "Modern nationalistic thought exercised a greater influence on the resistance ideologies of Muslim and Arab national liberation movements than anything in the Islamic tradition."

The Palestinians were and still are resisting Western powers' decision to give what they believe to be their land to the Jews.

That being said, I'm sure for some there are fundamental beliefs and cultural aspects of Islam that may have held them back from being respected as equal players in the world, but I think those variables play a much lesser role than the fact that we stole their land and gave it to the Jews.

We don't know what would have happened to the Muslim people if they were the ones forced out of their lands and made to survive in a Western society, benefiting from and participating hands-on in worldwide enlightenments, and then were handed sacred territory and were funded by superpowers. We don't know what would have happened if one of the major powers of the world had given them the support needed to build their own nation.

This leads us to another important factor: foreign aid.

In 2001, the year of 9/11, the conservative estimate of direct U.S. aid to Israel was almost $114 billion.

It's not easy to find foreign aid numbers, or to determine exactly how much the U.S. has devoted to Arab Muslim countries, but it is a known fact that no single Arab Muslim country has received the amount of substantial aid that Israel has received over the same time period.

To put this in better perspective, let's take a deeper look into U.S. foreign aid in 2001— again, before the worst terror attack on America.

The top three recipients of financial aid supplied by the United States in 2001 were as follows: Israel with $2.82 billion, followed by two out of three Israeli neighbors; $1.987 billion for Egypt, and $0.227 billion for Jordan.

A third of all foreign aid goes to Israel. Egypt also receives a significant amount of aid, mostly to protect Israel.

Now let's consider the relationships our country has with these countries.

Of course, we have close ties with Israel. The United States offers more than funding; it serves as one of the most powerful caucuses and lobbyists supporting the Jewish people in the whole world. And even though we're on decent (if sometimes tense) terms with Egypt and Jordan, those relationships are affected most of all by our strategic relationship with Israel. We keep dissident Egyptian and Jordanian voices at bay, for the most part, with funding, foreign aid, and security support.

There are more than a few Arab Muslim countries on our top 10 foreign aid lists, but not one receives even close to the amount of funding that is provided to the Jewish state of Israel. Note that the Palestinians were not on that top 10 list.

You might ask, why would the United States turn a blind eye to violations of our values and human rights by funding Arab dictators and waive sanctions for the same violations the Russians may exercise against regressive countries like Saudi Arabia?

Our apathy toward people who don't fit into our strategic foreign policy may explain things—9/11 being just one of many.

The mad animal we created—literally trained to kill (when we helped the Taliban fight the Soviets)—came after us when they figured out we didn't really care about them.

Once our selfish motives became evident, they turned on us, enraged.

Western countries have dominated and colonized much of the world, raping and pillaging the land, for centuries. Only recently— within the last 60-100 years or so (mostly post-World War II)—have we begun removing ourselves from the mess we created, using a rushed scalpel to perform a hurried surgical extrication.

It is important to note that as imperialism declined in Europe, the British, French, Spanish, and Portuguese pulled out of many of their foreign territories and sent very few troops into foreign wars, and that the U.S. used to be highly isolationist until WWI.

Just as the vast empires of Europe were in decline, the U.S. began inserting itself more into foreign affairs, but was hesitant to do so— even waiting two years to get involved in WWII.

There was a post-WWII mentality that increased U.S. involvement in foreign affairs, but it wasn't focused on colonization—quite the opposite. Franklin D. Roosevelt was the visionary behind anti-colonialism. But in too many cases, and seemingly with our support (after his death), there was a rush to hand power back to residents, which resulted in civil war, not to mention other damage.

Currently there are lingering commercial contracts whereby Western countries still dominate the national resources of once-colonized lands. Little of the money exchanging hands benefits the local communities. Too often profits that aren't siphoned off by ex-colonizers are slipped into the pockets of dictators.

When trends in de-colonization are considered, the anomaly of Israel becomes glaringly obvious. As more and more colonists withdrew from foreign lands and restored power to those previously oppressed, the League of Nations (which would become the United Nations) gave Israel to the Jews.

Why didn't we give Palestine back to the local Arabs?

It is my view that the British and the equivalent to the UN gave it to the Jews because of their connection to Abraham.

What other reason to choose a side than to give it to the brother with whom you have the closest ties?

Granted, Jewish rights to the land are ancient, but the fact of the matter is the Jews certainly did not have the majority demographic in Palestine at the time. In fact, fewer than 7-10 percent of Jews lived in Palestine at the time, meaning the land was occupied mostly by Palestinians when Western power gave the land to the Jews. The population was over 90 percent Palestinian, even after most of those Arabs fled to neighboring countries. There was a Palestinian diaspora, so the pain is felt deeply throughout the Middle East.

The original intention was this: Palestinians and the new Jewish state would share land and resources.

When that didn't work, the League of Nations (UN) cut loose and ran, sending money to Israel whenever needed. They essentially bought themselves a strategic Middle Eastern ally. It was seen as a defense of our oil and economic interests and a defense against the Russian influence in the region.

All of this makes me think of the old adage, "You reap what you sow," because we shaped the DNA Memory of the groups of people who now distrust and despise us.

What are we harvesting today?

CHAPTER 4 – Propaganda

"The man who wants to gain wisdom profits greatly from having thought for a time that man is basically evil and degenerate: this idea is wrong, like its opposite, but for whole periods of time it was predominant and its roots have sunk deep into us and into our world. To understand ourselves we must understand it; but to climb higher, we must then climb over and beyond it." — *Friedrich Nietzsche*

When I was in Egypt, I developed the habit of taking dinner at the same spot each night, daringly reading *God Is Not Great* by Christopher Hitchens. I started to notice that one of the servers was curious about me, so I made eye contact and asked him how he was. He seemed happy for the opportunity to talk.

"I am fine, thank you. Hey, you read a lot, huh? You always have that book in your hand."

This is how we became friends, with a simple smile and hello, much like what happened between me and the Catholic woman, and with my guide in Jerusalem.

He asked what I was doing in Sinai. I shared that I was working on a book, researching and studying a theory on DNA Memory, but also had come to take scuba lessons. He was used to people being there for scuba, clearly, because he smiled and said it's the best place to see colorful fish (although he admitted he had never taken a dive himself). He then jumped into asking me more questions, surprisingly interested in my project, but most intrigued by the fact that I was American.

He wanted some answers.

We met over the course of a few nights, after he got off work, each time spending a couple hours discussing various topics. His questions revealed as much about him as the things he shared with me. For example, he wanted to know why American movies always depict Muslims as angry and mean.

I explained to him that the U.S. film industry is by no means a real representation of what the people of the United States think and feel. However, I did admit that no doubt these movies affect people, especially those who have no contact with Muslims.

CHAPTER 4 – Propaganda

I told him that the ignorance that divides us is shaped by what people see in the news about the wars happening in the Middle East. It's not easy to keep up with the facts when all you're hearing is sound bites. To the detriment of our world at large, few people read the details written by qualified journalists in respectful newspapers. Even fewer travel to places where they could have contact and real experiences. These are mostly people trying, as he is, to survive, which requires working hard each day. When we are simply trying to survive, we don't pay as much attention to issues unrelated to our daily lives.

As a result, stereotypes take hold. This is true for all of us, regardless of what country we call home.

I asked him where he usually got his news. He said he went online and read mostly local newspapers. I asked, "Do you ever question if the information you are getting is correct?"

At that he paused a moment and said, "I don't know." To which I replied, "That could be what's happening in the United States, also. People don't always stop and consider that there are a few ways to look at a story, the so-called he said, she said of a situation."

Alternative facts are not facts. He understood this. We wholeheartedly agreed that the media contributes to the perception problem.

He wanted to know what I knew about Islam, so I went on to outline the following: "I understand that first came Judaism, then Christianity, and that Islam is the most recent of the monotheistic Abraham religions. I know it's one of the fastest-growing religions in the world. I know that Muslims believe Muhammad was their prophet. He was considered a simple man—a shepherd and a merchant. I also know that Muslims believe the angel Gabriel visited him and told him to read. At this point in time he could not read or write, but because it was demanded of him, he did. Historians say that much of what is in the Qur'an mirrors the Bible and Torah, and like the other monotheistic religions, Islam is based mostly on strong moral, ethical rules and encourages peace and just dealings; but like the other religions, has some dark stories, which could be interpreted in various ways.

Islam has no religious establishment—no popes or bishops telling people what to do. Islam also teaches that the earlier scriptures were sometimes lost or altered, and that a final prophet, Muhammad, completed God's message to humankind and hence the religion of Islam was born. But Islam is an oral tradition and it's not considered acceptable for it to be translated into any language other than the ancient Aramaic (unlike the Bible or the Torah.) And beyond that, the dialect of this ancient language is specific to the land where Muhammad was born—Mecca—therefore any translation can be difficult and may vary wildly.

I know that Mecca is also where Muhammad started his infamous journey, ending where the Temple of the Dome currently stands and where Muslims believe he rode his horse into heaven. I understand that traditional Muslims don't eat pork, much like the Jews, and avoid alcohol as well. I know there is a large group of African Americans and Asians who are Muslims (impacted by trade routes), which interests me a great deal, but that is another analysis for another conversation. I see and hear, via the minarets, that prayer is scheduled five times a day at 5 am, 12 pm, 3 pm, 5 pm and again at 7 pm, depending on the position of the sun..."

I could have kept going, but he stopped me, saying he was impressed. Then he asked me, "What do you think about my religion?"

This was a more difficult question.

I told him I was agnostic, adding I had a new definition for that which means I am open, curious, and harmonious, but not absolute. I joked that if someone were to look at the spectrum with fundamentalist, zealous religious people on one side and atheists and non-believers on the other side, that I sit somewhere in the middle of that spectrum—in a different universe.

I went on to explain that I sincerely respected his beliefs, as I respected the beliefs of any person, whatever they were, as long as they didn't violate inalienable human rights.

I shared that I am fascinated by how Islam spread around the world. Indonesian history is of considerable interest because it's full of contradictions. Such is the mix of Islam with Buddhism. In Indonesia, there are Muslim cross-dressers competing to be crowned Miss Indonesian Transvestite of the year who also pray in the women's section of the mosque while wearing the traditional headscarf.

The latter part of that passage made him laugh uncomfortably. He made it clear that he lives in a much different culture. Something stricter, more traditional.

I pressed, "I do have issues with any absolutist theory, on either side of the scale. I take issue when someone says they know absolutely 'this is truth' because, in my opinion, that's one of the main reasons that progress is stunted."

Then I asked him, "Is it true that from a young age, Muslims are taught not to ask questions?" He said, "That is true. It's easier that way." He and other Muslims explained to me that some religious teachings could be difficult to accept until you learn to have faith. I told him I had an issue with that way of thinking because "it teaches behavior that doesn't inspire the critical thinking needed to move beyond the status quo and to evolve."

He seemed to leave it be, even though he had a perfect chance to tell me other religions do the same thing. Instead he followed up with, "Do you believe in God?"

I gave him my standard answer. "I don't know if there is a god. As that ant on the ground doesn't know who I am, doesn't realize to what extent I exist—that I can't communicate with it and it can't communicate with me, though here I am and there it is. I am not so arrogant as to believe that there isn't a power or energy or whatever, something greater than me."

He laughed and said, "Your mind is big!" To which I replied, "Shukran! I think..." We laughed.

He did not question my logic, even if he did not agree with the conclusions my logic drew. I'm inclined to say he appreciated my agnostic philosophy, but maybe that is wishful thinking. Something made me feel comfortable with this young man, so I decided to change the subject and ask him point blank what he thought about the Jewish race being so incredibly advanced across a variety of disciplines.

"Well, Egyptians are very smart, too. We have won four Nobel Prizes," he said proudly, to which my response was, "Sure, and that is great, but let's run the numbers. Compare the population of Egypt (44 million) to the entire Jewish race (13 million)."

CHAPTER 4 – Propaganda

I then explained what I thought was the basic and general evolutionary history of the Jewish people and my theories about where they are today because of their oppression.

To this he literally took a step back. He was clearly surprised. He had never thought about these things, and I could tell he questioned my intentions a bit.

The look on his face could not hide the process going on inside his head, so I added, leaning forward, "Now, look, I'm not saying this because I think they are a superior race. I simply believe they have evolved, and quite interestingly they evolved into their current state because of how they were oppressed as a group of people."

I explained the big picture like this.

There are three brothers, each of which represent a generalized group of everyday people: Jews, Muslims, and Christians.

One brother, the Jew, was not allowed to own land and was kicked out of his homeland, forced out into the big bad world, surviving, for the most part by using his brain. In doing so, the Jewish brother became an exceptional problem solver of modern issues because this was how he had to make a living, and this is what his culture has encouraged him to do. This brother loved his family and his culture, and he maintained it well, trusting those like him more than anyone else, because, over time, his oppression gave him trust issues. He harbored a lot of fear because people outside his community didn't like him and went out of their way to hurt him.

The other brother—the Muslim brother—had a much different struggle for survival. He owned land or lived a nomadic life where he and his family and community lived on great landmasses. This brother had unfortunate and terrible fights with his neighbors over limited natural resources. He also faced other struggles related to power. The fights continued, but for the most part he lived off the land well enough, building bigger and bigger families, spreading quickly and keeping a rather uncomplicated life.

The daily struggle, in different ways, continued for the two brothers up until the recent modern day. Until the Jews, as a group of people, were attack by a horrible agent.

Reluctantly the third brother—the Christian brother—came in to save and protect the Jews. Once the fight was won, the Jews needed a place and time to heal. So, the Christian brother decided to give the first brother land.

The Muslim brother was living in the area the Christian brother was occupying, when all of sudden the Christian brother decided to give the land he had occupied not to the Muslim brother, but to the Jewish brother.

For reasons the Muslim brother doesn't understand, the outside world seems to favor the Jewish brother taking the land as his own.

A fight started, this time between the Jewish and the Muslim brothers, so the Christian brother decided to step out of the arena, and instead of throwing punches himself, he chose to fund one side of the fight—namely, that of the Jewish brother.

The anger grew until finally the brother who never left—the Muslim brother—began screaming to the rest of the world that this was not fair, that their land is called Palestine. They do not believe their land is Israel. They do not believe it should be owned by the Jewish brother. They do not believe the Christian brother has the right to give their land to the Jewish brother. The land belongs to them, the Muslim brother.

But the Jewish brother moved in anyway and began to build, and build, and build until finally he had established one of the most powerful nations in the world. As this happened, the Muslim brother's quality of life deteriorated and his anger toward the Jewish and Christian brothers escalated.

The Jewish brother believes the land once called Palestine is now Israel. He is convinced that it is rightfully his, so the Jewish brother gathers all his advanced knowledge of the modern world and uses it against the Muslim brother.

Cutting-edge warfare is waged. A new breed of terrorism is born.

The Muslim brother did not have the advanced tools and weapons like his Jewish brethren and, feeling angry and desperate, did what he could to fight back. Palestine, in his eyes, is his land— a birthright.

From here we see the roots of modern terrorism. We see how the Muslim brother felt cornered and why he fought back. We also see that the Jewish brother, who has been oppressed, feels he has the right to the land and peace at long last, and why the Jewish brother fights back.

Extreme measures are taken to secure the Jewish state by the Christian brother. The war not only continues to this day, but also is evolving into something earth-shattering.

The result? Palestinians live in third-world conditions. Israel is becoming more and more powerful, but instead of leading peacefully, it's approaching a nuclear war—a standoff with the bigger, stronger brothers in Iran—and a nefarious outsider called Russia whose oil/military influence in the region is felt by all.

Arab Muslim nations like Iran are coming to the defense of the Palestinians. And of course, when push comes to shove, Western allies (and their beneficiaries) will come to the defense of Israel. With this we a have similar combination of variables and factors to those that brought about previous world wars.

I stopped my explanation here. We sat quietly for a moment. He broke our silence, saying he thought the story "fairly described" what is happening.

After a pause, I asked him, "So, what's next?"

He didn't know, because none of us know.

He said he wants peace. And he did say that Jews and Muslims used to be able to get along and he hopes that can happen. He told stories of how his father used to work with Jews.

We sat quietly again.

I silently considered important questions. Where do we find compromise? Who is willing to let go and/or give, and of what? How do we avoid a third world war?

My new friend was quiet as he also contemplated the story. I could sense he didn't know what to say. I decided to change the subject and asked him some personal questions. I knew he was expecting his first child, and sadly his wife was in Cairo, more than five hours away. He took care of his family, like many men in Egypt do, from a distance. He was looking forward to leaving work to make his monthly visit, but his manager was making him stay, even though she was due soon. I took the opportunity to talk about something I knew mattered to him—his child.

I asked, "Don't you want a better quality of life for your child?"

He was a bit offended. "My family has a good quality of life!"

I backpedaled a bit, saying, "Yes, I know, you work hard and support your family well. You work six to seven days a week, all day long, with little break, yes?" He nodded. "You see your family maybe a few days a month, yes?" He said, "That's right."

"And to be fair, you could say these living conditions are not easy, agreed?"

"We have a simple, happy life," he replied.

Encouraged, I continued, "But doesn't every parent want a better life for their child?"

He was quiet again as he waited for me to continue. "You have a good enough job, so imagine how much harder it is for other families who were not as lucky as yours, or even all the families that are like yours. Are you happy with your educational and health systems, with the pollution that is all around? Do you believe you have a fair opportunity to better your quality of life?"

He finally conceded by saying, "I understand your point."

"Look," I said. "The Middle Eastern Muslims and the Jews—Western power, too—all can continue or escalate this war, or we can simply understand and accept—with humility—how we got to this point. Then we can move on from the past and make better decisions to positively impact our futures together.

There is no going back. We can only move forward. Israel is a powerful economic force, a good—though not perfect—example of a solid democracy in the Middle East. Why not partner with them? Demand of them, peacefully, to learn from their own history and to help the Palestinians achieve a healthier, fairer, better quality of life."

CHAPTER 4 – Propaganda

He humored me by continuing to listen with a friendly smirk on his face, so I went on to give examples of how people in third-world countries are as capable of producing intellectual results on the scale of the Jewish people in a very short period of time.

I cited President Obama as an example. I told him that it was only a couple of generations ago that Obama's grandfather lived in a rural environment—as a local leader, yes, but an uncomplicated one, as a shepherd. Not that there is anything wrong with that, but the point is, it's possible to make the leap, in a few generations, to the level of President of the United States of America.

He liked this idea, but said, "I am a simple man. A holy man. I can't change my country. I must take care of my family. It's expensive to have a family. I must work."

"Well, somebody needs to make a stand," I said. "If the United States never had Martin Luther King, we wouldn't have President Obama. There must be a Muslim somewhere in the Arab world who is thinking about these things and taking a lead for peace.

We went back and forth on more cultural issues and what he says are the "misunderstandings" in regards to women's rights and more. I promised I'd read more about it, and I have.

Just as it's true we have various denominations of Christianity who interpret the Bible in ways that have different impacts on women, it is true that Muslims and Jews do as well. He is on the moderate part of the spectrum.

Although I agree more than ever that many Muslim women are not treated poorly, I pushed a little more. "I believe—and Obama mentioned in his discussion in Cairo—that women are critical to the overall development of Muslim communities, which means they, too, require the best of educational opportunities."

He didn't think his wife needed to go to college, so we retired the topic.

He wrapped up our question-and-answer series with a final question.

"Do you believe in destiny?"

CHAPTER 5 – Provocateurs

"In dreams begins responsibility."
— *William Butler Yeats*

The question about destiny sent me back to a moment in Jerusalem.

I had a chance meeting with another writer while waiting to go up to the Temple Mount. I planned to meet my guide and friend for a second time and for our last day together, but I got delayed in a very slow line.

"Do you know when they close the Temple Mount?"

I was a bit startled when this question was directed to me because I was lost in thought after standing quietly in line for so long. I responded slowly, saying, "No, sorry, I don't, but I know we have only a brief time to walk the grounds before prayer begins again."

He looked at me for a second, then asked, "Where you from?"

Again, the question-and-answer series.

He was from Los Angeles, too, and was also writing a book, although his was about the Bible. He said he believed he could prove, more than ever, that the Bible is 100 percent accurate, that each word is the perfect word of God.

He had been studying the Hebrew text, which he said is the only believable version (though he used a translation tool). He believed he had discovered a way to map various Biblical events precisely. That was why he was in Jerusalem. I assume this newly understood map is what his book is all about, but he didn't want to say.

Our conversation continued through the security line, which was nice because talking with him helped pass the time.

As we broke free from the prolonged process, he picked up his pace, expecting me to listen and follow, so I did, and we ended up— ironically enough—right where my Muslim friend took me the first time, where we made our prayer for peace.

He said, in clear enough terms, that there will be a third world war, that the Jewish people will build a third temple—as the Bible says—on the same spot where the current Temple of the Dome stands. He made sure I understood that "the Bible must be 100 percent accurate, because if not, it is 100 percent wrong."

This man reminded me of the dangerous nature of zealous belief, of fundamentalism—no matter what religious base it has.

If we've learned anything, we've learned that thoughts can manifest into action.

It was the first time on this journey where I felt like my hope was fading because an absolute point of view is hard to penetrate with fresh thinking.

He was so different from the Catholic nun, my Muslim guide, or my Egyptian friend. All the other people I had the pleasure to spend time with in the Old City and beyond resisted the use of absolutist words, instead preferring or focusing on the desire for peace.

After a while this man began to catch on that I held a different worldview than he did.

Suddenly he stopped, gave me a funny look, and said, "I don't know why I'm talking to you. I've been coming to Jerusalem a few times a year and never tell people these things."

He expressed strong negative perceptions about Muslims, believing their religion was made up and straight-up wrong. He questioned everyone that didn't believe 100 percent in the Bible.

I didn't know what to say in response. I felt this man was dangerous because of his lack of tolerance or willingness to let go in order for all of us to live and let live. But I knew I had to keep listening, to try and connect with him.

When I shared this story with the service worker in Egypt, I explained to him that the Christian man spoke about a third world war in absolute terms. And after a pause, I answered his question about destiny, "I believe it's up to us to envision the world we want to live in."

CONCLUSION

"I've learned that people will forget what you said, people will forget what you did, but people will never forget how you made them feel."
— Maya Angelou

Our current Zoe is imprinting more fear and hate into our global culture and into our Bios for generations to come. More than ever, we need a wise pivot towards peace and compassion. It's up to the secular and democratic citizens of the world to take notice and get engaged, particularly in the United States of America.

Because far right wing and radicalized religious people have a blurred lens, we must step in to help.

I now understand why Christopher Hitchens took the position that religion is abhorrent. When you look at the details laid out in his book *God is not Great* (the same book I was reading and finished in Egypt when the server caught my eye), you get a sense of where his superior attitude comes from. Many terrible acts have been done in the name of God; surely, we should know better. But we must also remember that glorious acts of love are also at the core of the Abrahamic religions.

People in power in the United States and across Western society have twisted what it means to be Christian. The Muslims are not alone in fighting back the infection of fear and hate in their communities. And Israel is struggling as well.

It's heartbreaking to realize how much damage has been done and how the saga continues. The traumatizing DNA Memory, like PTSD (post-traumatic stress disorder), is being compounded in the oppressed. And the oppressors in the world are only serving to hurt all of us by digging this unsustainable trench. It can truly seem like a dead end.

But pointing fingers and telling people they are wrong for seeing the world the way they do is not only insulting, but also futile. Making people feel inferior is self-defeating. It's a tragic expression of our own ancient resentment.

I believe that I was able to connect with people because they could see I was truly listening and open instead of fixated on my own perceptions and agenda.

That is where this theory of DNA Memory and my study of epigenetics has helped me. Originally, I had planned a trip to follow my own DNA Memory. I hired a professional genealogist and took DNA tests to track where my family came from. I explored my history, looking into factors that influenced their lives and contemplating how the experiences of my ancestors made me who I was and have become. While on my personal journey, I became intrigued by the stories of others. I traveled to and passed through 13 countries and talked to countless people.

There is no more compelling and impactful story than this in terms of global impact.

I see the heart of the Middle East beating strong. Its pulse is throbbing, felt around the world. But it's been working too hard for too long, and now the entire region is struggling. Its critical state is such that if it doesn't rest and heal soon, the consequences will be dire for all of us. We can't afford to let the situation worsen.

As I write this, there are ICE raids happening in Los Angeles creating panic and terror in families, too many of whom were born here, have no criminal background and simply entered our golden door because, like my immigrant family, they sought liberty and prosperity.

The U.S. Court of Appeals for the 9th Circuit unanimously denied the government's request to lift a nationwide injection on what amounts to a Muslim ban. Not only are we traumatizing Muslim Americans, we're reinforcing the enemies' narrative in the hearts and minds of Muslims around the world.

As all of this happens, we seem to be ignoring once again that police are killing unarmed black and brown men and women at grossly disproportionate rates. White privilege and racism continues to strike and strike hard.

What DNA Memory are we imprinting when we emotionally bomb these communities? What result do we expect?

I've learned along this DNA Memory trek that many if not all things are somewhat connected. Israel is a cross section of ancient, post-modern, and cutting edge. For me, it feels like home, despite being neither Jewish nor Arab. I imagine my people passed through the cradle of Israel. Its imprint is in me as well.

I didn't know where this trek would take me, but it's clearer now. It's time to reevaluate our approach and clear our lens. And time is of the essence. We can use it constructively.

We can better understand the nature of the people in each battle and how hundreds if not thousands of years have led us to this moment, but that history doesn't need to—and must not—define tomorrow.

The policies of segregation and division lead us into no-win situations.

Therefore, it is my hope that we can use this theory of DNA Memory to fight for a unifying understanding of different religions as we support different multiracial cultures and lifestyles.

The foundational question is: how can we imprint peace rather than instigate terrorism?

I call upon Americans and Western society to imagine a better path forward for all of us. Why? Because human dignity and freedom are not things we vote on—they are inalienable rights. They are in every human/Bios constitution, not just written on parchment paper. We must accept this fact as the foundation for all decisions moving forward.

We must invest in "We the People."

I believe this starts with providing the means for healthcare and education. That is where secular and democratic society can step in. No matter what our personal beliefs may be, certainly we can agree that all children and families deserve to live healthy lives and be well-educated.

To be healthy means to not be afraid and to have equal access to services without going into debt. To educate means to value our true history and offer all people in all places the best available resources to get ahead.

We must not turn away. This is our moment to empower those who are willing to shift the battle from terror to a peaceful understanding.

This will require sustained effort. In order to embrace into prosperity those who are like us, pursuing happiness and peace, we must participate in and improve not only our political infrastructure but also, more importantly, our culture. That is how we improve our Zoe, which will imprint a better DNA Memory into our Bios.

We must push back against unjust laws using non-violent measures. Only then will peace triumph.

It's in our best interests to help the people living in third-world environments, developing countries, and the ghettos in our backyards to get on a level playing field. We must empower all these people to control their own destinies.

It's the best investment toward peace and a broader competitive economy. I propose this is the path to a better economy with a strong middle class.

To this end, our foreign aid should match our desired outcome.

Today—after declaring war following September 11th, 2001—Jordan and Iraq received roughly equal amounts of military aid, with Pakistan not far behind. It's basically the same investment that led us to our current position. In terms of economic aid, Israel received by far the most, followed by Egypt, then Afghanistan, and then Jordan in fourth place, not third like in 2001.

We're funding terror globally, and with this new President of the United States, we're expanding the effort domestically.

Our short-term fight is already happening as we see the direct action and protests unfold across the U.S. and the world—in our streets and in our town halls. We must continue to demand a transparent democracy, free media, and free speech so everyone can engage in civic participation. This is essential if we are to educate our population about the true problems we face, giving each of us the tools necessary to make a difference in our local arenas.

We cannot back down from the truth that facts matter. It is essential that we own our history and recognize the fact that the things our leaders do have lasting impact. We must call on them to make the right decisions in terms of our foreign and domestic policy.

CONCLUSION

I want our leaders to know that we need them to support Israel, with the expectation that my dear Jewish friends will help others in need and become a role model and a hub for development across the Middle East.

My wish is that they resist nationalistic thinking and come to heal themselves of the infection of war, all the while recognizing that each new settlement is a move toward one state, fully integrated with the Palestinians—not fostering more segregation.

I worry that we're past the point of a two-state solution. And although I recognize that the Arab population will outnumber the Jewish and understand why that is a scary thought for many, I firmly believe that human dignity is required if we are to achieve freedom and prosperity for all. We must forge a new way forward.

These same principles guide me and are the reason why I ask our leaders to support the Palestinians and Muslims around the globe as well.

My wish is that Muslim communities will inspire a revolutionary leader, the likes of

Martin Luther King Jr., to lead them into a peaceful, mutually beneficial solution and integrate with the Israelis in a completely new and innovative way.

The lessons of slavery and oppression in the United States taught us that segregation is a losing matter for all involved, which is why I support a nation where equal rights prevail.

I recognize Israel's right to exist mostly because we need a strong model of a democratic state in the Middle East. We must encourage the people of Israel to get creative in how they leverage their new and profound power in the world—for the public good.

Middle Eastern leaders must cultivate a fresh relationship with Israel and the rest of the world. It is my hope that they aspire to evolve into the modern way of life, in a way that makes sense for them and emboldens them to take their rightful, blessed place at the round table.

Americans have a responsibility. We should approach the Muslim and Arab communities with empathy and help them believe that a better life is attainable in a democratic and secular society.

The evolution of DNA Memory from these most vulnerable groups of people, especially in Israel and the surrounding Arab Muslim developing communities, might constitute an intersectional tipping point.

Imagine a world where our tax dollars focus on the health and education of our children instead of the regressive military complex we have today. This will have significant implications for our children and families— people living in the United States—and planet Earth.

This doesn't mean we don't have real threats in the world we need to defend against. Terrorism won't go away overnight and, in fact, is evolving into bio-terrorism. Cyberwarfare is real. Nuclear stockpiling and nefarious testing are happening.

So, I leave you with this. Mahatma Gandhi said something which turned into a bumper sticker, "Be the change you want to see in the world." I argue that is not enough in this pivotal moment, and that is not all that he said.

We must understand why people do what they do before we can make change in the world. It's not enough to model or ask for change because modern society currently lives in an echo chamber and within its own ideological social media bubbles.

The rules of engagement have changed. We must accept the new tensions, push forward, and take action in new ways. We must accept that the needs of the most vulnerable communities require more than a peace agreement.

This effort is about our culture, the Zoe in which we live, and our Bios, the matter we want to share with our kids.

The responsibility is on us because it's our decision to make. Will we let terrorism dominate our DNA Memory and define our quality of life now and in the future? Or will we come to realize that true peace requires an equitable chance at life for all of us?

I vote for the latter.

Works Referenced

(not all sources are listed):

Carey, N. (2013). *The Epigenetics Revolution – How Modern Biology Is Rewriting Our Understanding of Genetics, Disease, and Inheritance*. New York: Columbia University Press.

Korczak, J. (2009). Summary of Geographical Movement of European Jews in the Past 2,000 Years. Retrieved April 24, 2017, from http://fcit.usf.edu/holocaust/People/displa ce.htm, University of South Florida

Spiro, K., Rabbi. (2001, November 24). History Crash Course #53: The Enlightenment. Retrieved April 24, 2017, from http://www.aish.com/jl/h/48955286.html

Brooks, D. (2010, January 11). The Tel Aviv Cluster. Retrieved April 24, 2017, from http://www.nytimes.com/2010/01/12/opin ion/12brooks.html, New York Times

WEISS, A. (2016). State of the Nation Report, Society, Economy and Policy in Israel. Retrieved from http://taubcenter.org.il/wp-content/files_mf/stateofthenation2016.pdf

Can Islam and Democracy coexist? (2007). Retrieved April 24, 2017, from http://www.pbs.org/weta/crossroads/about/show_indonesia.html, PBS

Mabrouk, M. F. (2016, July 28). Thoughts on President Obama's Cairo Speech | Brookings Institution. Retrieved April 24, 2017, from https://www.brookings.edu/opinions/thoughts-on-president-obamas-cairo-speech/Brookings

President Obama Speaks to the Muslim World from Cairo, Egypt. (2009, June 04). Retrieved April 24, 2017, from https://www.youtube.com/watch?v=6BlqLwCKkeY, The White House

Politics and Economy. (n.d.). Retrieved April 24, 2017, from http://www.laits.utexas.edu/cairo/modern/

business/business.html The University of Texas at Austin
Reaction: Obama's Cairo speech. (2009, June 04). Retrieved April 24, 2017, from http://news.bbc.co.uk/2/hi/8083171.stmBC

McArthur, S. (2009, July 20). Congress Watch: A Conservative Estimate of Total Direct U.S. Aid to Israel: Almost $114 Billion - Telling the truth for more than 30 years. Retrieved April 24, 2017, from http://www.washingtonreport.me/2008-november/congress-watch-a-conservative-estimate-of-total-direct-u.s.-aid-to-israel-almost-$114-billion.html, The American Educational Trust (AET)

Katz, R. N. (2009, June 30). Obama Increasing Aid to Jordan, Other Muslim States. Retrieved April 24, 2017, from http://www.israelnationalnews.com/News/News.aspx/132131, Arutz Sheva 7

Slackman, M. (2009, February 18). Egyptian Political Dissident, Imprisoned for Years, Is Suddenly Released. Retrieved April 24, 2017, from http://www.nytimes.com/2009/02/19/worl

d/middleeast/19egypt.htmlNew York Times

Aly, A. M. (2009, April 28). Iran's New Target: Egypt. Retrieved April 24, 2017, from https://www.wsj.com/articles/SB12408739 4756961155Wall Street Journal

Bruno, G. (2011, October 13). State Sponsors: Iran. Retrieved April 24, 2017, from http://www.cfr.org/iran/state-sponsors-iran/p9362Council on Foreign Relations
Congressional Budget Justification: FOREIGN ASSISTANCE. (2015). Retrieved from https://www.state.gov/documents/organiz ation/224071.p

Learn more, go to: ZoeBios.com

About the Author

Katie Smith is a first-time author and an amateur humanist philosopher who, in 2009, took an 18-month sabbatical to travel and work, alone or in artist residencies across 13 countries, to trace down her family's DNA Memory. Zoe Bios originated as a poetic interpretation of epigenetics and a way to explain her theory of DNA Memory. This book is the product of a decade's worth of research and discussion.

She spends her days as a communications strategist who has worked with ACLU National, Advancement Project California, USA for UNHCR, Calvert Foundation, Common Sense Media, and other innovative organizations seeking effective ways to defend our civil rights and assert a progressive agenda.

Ms. Smith was born and raised in Los Angeles.

ZoeBios.com

69553932R00066

Made in the USA
San Bernardino, CA
17 February 2018